LOOKING AT PAINTINGS

Seascapes

The Whirlpools of Awa
Andō Hiroshige. Color woodcut on paper, 1855

LOOKING AT PAINTINGS

Seascapes

Peggy Roalf

Series Editor
Jacques Lowe

Designer
Amy Hill

Hyperion Books for Children

A
JACQUES LOWE
VISUAL ARTS PROJECTS
BOOK

Text Copyright © 1992 by Jacques Lowe Visual Arts Projects Inc.

Printed in Italy

FIRST EDITION

1   3   5   7   9   10   8   6   4   2

Library of Congress Cataloging-in-Publication Data

Roalf, Peggy.

Seascapes/Peggy Roalf — 1st ed.

p. cm — (Looking at paintings)

"A Jacques Lowe Visual Arts projects book"—T.p. verso.

Summary: Examines seascapes by noted painters in a variety of techniques.

ISBN 1-56282-093-1 (trade) — ISBN 1-56282-094-X (lib. bdg.)

1. Sea in art—Juvenile literature. 2. Marine painting—Juvenile literature.

[1. Sea in art. 2. Marine painting. 3. Painting—History. 4. Art appreciation.]

I. Title. II. Series: Roalf, Peggy. Looking at paintings.

ND1370.R6 1992

758'.2—dc20   91–74079

CIP

AC

Contents

Introduction

*L*OOKING AT PAINTINGS is a series of books about understanding what great artists see when they paint. Painters have been drawn to the mysterious power of the sea for more than two thousand years. Some artists have painted heroic naval battles. Some show us how forceful storms have directed the lives of people who work on the sea. Others have expressed the magical interplay of sky and water in colors that never occur on land. By looking at many paintings of this one subject, we can see how artists have used their talent and imagination to bring their own experience of the sea to life.

Painters often invent revolutionary techniques—or combine unusual images—to express their vision. Long ago, Pieter Brueghel the Elder combined a sky, an ocean, and ships he had seen in Italy with the countryside of Flanders to create an enchanted scene in *Landscape with the Fall of Icarus*. Joseph Mallord William Turner captured a moment when the sky, water, and land dissolve into a mist of luminous color by allowing the naturally watery qualities of watercolor paint to guide him in *Tours Sunset*. When Turner painted *The Whale Ship,* he used rags, scrapers, and brush handles to stir up the texture of a turbulent sea into the oil paint—and created an image of the conflict between man and nature.

Artists transform what they see into images that take us on a journey to other times and to distant places. You can learn to observe the power and the beauty of an ocean, a river, or a lake—and use your imagination to see like a painter.

A SANCTUARY BY THE SEA, 20 B.C.–A.D. 45
Third Pompeiian Style, Unknown Roman Artist, Fresco, detail 20½" x 24⅜"

*P*ompeii, a prosperous city with a rich cultural life, was obliterated when Mount Vesuvius erupted in A.D. 79. The volcano buried the city under a deep layer of molten lava, and Pompeii vanished from memory until its ruins were unearthed in 1748. The lava had preserved buildings, paintings, objects, and even the people by sealing out air. Archaeologists have slowly pieced Pompeii back together to understand the life of the ancient city.

Merchants, bankers, and wealthy landowners of Pompeii lived in well-designed houses decorated with elaborate wall paintings such as this one. Decorative painting was a professional trade, run by master artists who created designs and supervised artisans, who did much of the work. The artisan applied a layer of wet plaster in an area small enough to complete in one session, then painted into the fresh plaster using pigments mixed with water. Because the paint bonded with wet plaster, the finished surface was hard and durable. Finally, the painting was polished to a smooth, gleaming finish.

The limited colors in this seascape—black, white, green, and brown—create a peaceful mood. Water and sky are painted a mottled black to imitate a precious marble prized for its beauty. Details in the boats, the ripples on the water, and the misty pavilion in the background are painted with great delicacy. The seated figure contemplating the quiet lagoon adds to the air of tranquillity in this graceful mural. Even though cracks have damaged its surface, we can look at this painting and imagine the splendid room it once decorated.

The Roman artist shaped a graceful boat with earth-colored paint. A few touches of white separate the boat from the dark water.

8

NAVAL BATTLE, 1520
From *Commentaries on the Gallic Wars*, Volume 3
Godefroy le Batave, Dutch, Watercolor on vellum, 8" x 5"

King Francis I was loved by the people of France. He traveled to every corner of the kingdom to meet the peasants as well as the nobles. In 1520, when France was surrounded by enemies ready to attack by sea, the ghost of the great Roman emperor Julius Caesar appeared to Francis. Francis asked the ghost how Caesar, in his time, had created peace through military victory. Fifteen hundred years earlier, Caesar had conquered France, then known as Gaul, and brought peace to its warring tribes. The king believed that this conversation was real, and that Caesar's words helped him in battle. Later that year, Francis commissioned an artist and a writer to record the dialogue in an *illuminated manuscript* — a handmade, illustrated book.

On one page of the book, Godefroy le Batave depicted a battle at sea. First, he painted the entire picture in pale gray watercolor. Over this, Godefroy shaped the pounding waves with azure blue and white paint, adding details in black. Using his skill in perspective drawing, he brought the scene to life by creating a great ocean space. In the foreground, the ships are large and detailed. They are smaller in the middle and become sketchy little outlines at the horizon.

The picture on this page shows the entire page of the manuscript, with its decorated initial *D*. Godefroy framed the painting with a gold border, and also used gold paint for the beautiful hand-drawn lettering. The art of the illuminated manuscript vanished when the invention of the printing press made books available in large quantities. But this book is still treasured by the people of France as a great work of art, and in memory of Francis I, who spent twenty-eight years protecting his beloved country from invaders.

The gold and blue lettering on the manuscript repeats the conversation Francis I believed he had with the ghost of Julius Caesar: "King Francis asked Caesar how he won naval battles in his time. Caesar answered, 'Only with the greatest preparation.'"

11

LANDSCAPE WITH THE FALL OF ICARUS, 1567
Pieter Brueghel the Elder, Flemish (1525/30?–69),
Transferred from panel to canvas, 29" x 44"

*P*ieter Brueghel's life and art were formed by his belief in the cycles of nature: birth and death, the alternating seasons, the turning of the earth around the sun. He thought that people who tampered with natural forces were doomed, and in this painting he retold an ancient Greek story that illustrates his beliefs.

Daedalus, a legendary artist and inventor, became a prisoner of the evil King Midas on the island of Crete. Daedalus searched for an escape. There was no way out, until he realized that Midas could not control the sky. Daedalus fashioned wings of feathers, wax, and string for himself and for Icarus, his young son. With a warning to Icarus to stay close, he led their flight. But Icarus soon realized what fun it was to fly. He left his father behind, soaring higher and higher until the sun melted his wings and he fell into the sea.

Brueghel had traveled to Italy, making drawings of the ocean, the cities, and the mountains along the way. In this painting, he used features from different regions to suit his vision of the natural world. In sweeping arcs of blue and green, he created the sea and sky in the shimmering image of the Mediterranean. The great ship with its billowing sails is the kind built in Venice at the time. The landscape, the farmers, the plants, and the animals are typical of Flanders, Brueghel's own country.

An old Flemish saying that encourages hard work also inspired Brueghel: "No plow stops over the death of any man." The farmer and fishermen go about their daily labor. The shepherd checks the sky to calculate the weather. Poor Icarus slips without notice into the water, making a tiny splash. And Daedalus, still soaring through the sky, is not even shown in the painting.

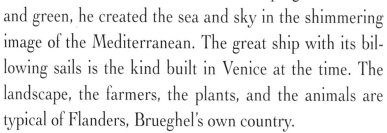

This detail shows how Brueghel made Icarus's disappearance seem unimportant by showing only a tiny splash and the boy's desperately kicking legs.

SEAPORT WITH ULYSSES RETURNING CHRYSEIUS TO HER FATHER, about 1644

Claude Lorrain (born Gellée), French (1600–1682), Oil on canvas, 46¼" x 59"

As a young man, Claude Gellée left his home in Lorraine, France, for Rome, to work as a chef. He was enchanted by the golden light that drenched the Roman countryside. Claude became a painter instead, and created visions of a tranquil world filled with shimmering light.

The *Iliad*, an epic composed by the Greek poet Homer about twenty-five hundred years earlier, inspired Claude to create this painting. In a battle against the Trojans, Ulysses had captured Chryseius, the beautiful daughter of a priest. Here, Ulysses has just returned Chryseius to her father, and prepares to set out for another battle. His great ship looms over the harbor, an eerie black presence against the brilliant sky.

Claude unified this busy scene with late-afternoon light. The sun, low in the sky, casts deep shadows across marble pavilions and darkens the foreground, creating a dreamlike atmosphere. The blue-black water ripples with silvery reflections that visually connect the pier and the ship. Claude's use of perspective in the painting is faulty—the building on the right seems to float above the water, and the ship tilts up at an odd angle. But he makes the space in this picture believable by emphasizing the luminous sky that invites Ulysses to cast off from the safe harbor.

Claude used the technique of aerial perspective. Figures in the foreground are clearly defined with strong colors, highlights, and shadows. Details and colors become softer in the middle, dissolving into a mist of translucent light at the horizon. Claude created the effect of a great space receding to an endless horizon.

Claude painted precise and colorful details in the foreground. We can identify Ulysses by his silky-looking red robe and great sword.

15

THE WHALE SHIP, about 1845

Joseph Mallord William Turner, English (1775–1851). Oil on canvas,
36¹/₈" x 48¹/₄"

J. M. W. Turner's father encouraged his son to become an artist. He displayed "Billy's" pictures in his London barbershop for his customers to purchase. At the age of fourteen, young Turner began his training, and he became a member of the prestigious Royal Academy of Arts at twenty-four.

At a time when seascape paintings were appreciated as accurate *pictures* of nature, Turner used his imagination to portray his own vision of *nature's power* over man. He re-created the effects of color and light with his unusual oil painting technique. Turner used every tool at hand, including house painters' brushes, rags, and palette knives, which were ordinarily used to mix paint. Turner often stirred up textures in the thick layers of paint with the wooden handles of his brushes.

This painting could almost be called a "skyscape." Turner has used two-thirds of the canvas to express the limitless horizon and the oppressive heat he imagined bearing down on the whaling ship. At the top of the painting, he shows the sun behind the white light of the cloud cover.

Instead of creating a typical sea-green ocean, Turner painted yellow reflections of the burning sun on the water. Streaks of paint form a great splash where the whale has breached out of the churning sea. The vast sky and the heroic size of the whale make the ship with its flapping sails and invisible crew seem helpless. For Turner, paint had its own reality, and fantastic pictures were hidden in the magical material. With slashing strokes of brush and palette knife, he translated the power of the sea into colors and textures to release the hidden images.

F. H. Brueghel created a fanciful scene in which a harpist tames three whales with music as the Dutch fleet prepares for battle.

TOURS SUNSET, about 1832
Joseph Mallord William Turner, English (1775–1851), Bodycolor on blue paper,
5¼" x 7½"

*E*very summer, Turner went on sketching tours of France, Switzerland, and Italy. He created descriptive paintings of popular tourist sites that were bought by travelers before postcards were available. But his vision was driven by light and color. He was excited by the way watercolor paint came to life on paper even before he had formed a picture. Guided by the flowing, changing nature of the watercolor itself, Turner developed a revolutionary technique.

Turner created a fantasy of the moment when the colors of sky, water, and earth appear to blend together. Using opaque paints thinned with water, he applied brilliant, transparent colors that he allowed to run together on the wet blue paper—and let large areas of paper show through for the sky and water. The bridge, buildings, and rock formations melt into a lavender haze that he created by removing paint with blotting paper. While the paper was still wet, he washed in a cloud of yellow for the sky and added earth-colored reflections that dissolve into the river. With opaque paint, Turner intensified the red sky, the blazing yellow sun, and their reflections on the water. Because he trusted his vision and his materials, Turner worked rapidly and his colors remained fresh and gemlike.

Some art critics in Turner's time appreciated careful craftsmanship more than imagination and creativity. They denounced Turner's new paintings as garish blotches and scribbles. Turner ignored these comments and continued to express his personal vision in hundreds of luminous watercolors.

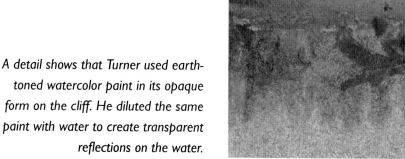

A detail shows that Turner used earth-toned watercolor paint in its opaque form on the cliff. He diluted the same paint with water to create transparent reflections on the water.

LAKE LEMAN AT SUNSET, 1875
Gustave Courbet, French (1819–1877), Oil on canvas, 29¹/₈" x 39³/₈"

Gustave Courbet was a radical in life and in art. He faced nature as it was—powerful, difficult, and not always pretty. He translated the democratic ideals of the French Revolution into paintings of ordinary working people. People who preferred paintings of idealized situations found Courbet's work shocking and crude.

After France was defeated in the Franco-Prussian War, the Paris Commune was established to restore democracy. Courbet became involved in a political intrigue. He was arrested, and then exiled to Switzerland.

In this painting, Courbet expressed the anguish that he felt at being separated forever from his beloved friends and country. A great bank of clouds seems like a wall blocking his view of France, across the lake. A boat is becalmed on the lake, its fragile-looking sails flapping in the still air. Flaming colors engulf the scene, like an inferno.

Courbet said that because nature is dark until the sun rises, he would paint nature by turning on the light with colors. He created the blazing effects of a sunset by painting brilliant colors over dark tones. Courbet allowed the dark reddish brown underpainting to show through—the darkest tones can be seen at the horizon. He thickened the bright red paint with sand to build up textures that imitate the appearance of waves, and created bright reflections on the water with dashes of pure white paint.

At the end of his life, Courbet was lonely and impoverished; but his view of nature inspired the next generation of French painters. Among them, Monet, Derain, and Gauguin saw the future of painting in Courbet's vision, and they would create the next revolution in art.

The seventeenth-century Dutch artist Ludolf Backhuyzen diluted ink with water to create the cloud formations. With the point of his brush, he painted the ship's rigging and flags in precise detail.

21

IMPRESSION, 1872
Claude Monet, French (1840–1926), Oil on canvas, 19⅞" x 25¾"

Claude Monet observed that the still water of Le Havre harbor was an enormous reflector. It bounced the colors of the sunset onto the surrounding ships and buildings. The orange sun dissolved the details of buildings in a fog of rusty color. Ships seemed to be the same cool, grayish lavender as the sky behind the setting sun. A skiff with two sailors became a deep blue silhouette against the strong light.

Monet used color instead of traditional perspective to create this picture of a harbor at sunset. He had observed in nature that warm colors such as yellow, orange, and red appear to come forward in space. Cool colors such as blue, purple, and green seem to recede. He used this knowledge to develop a new way of picturing space and light. Monet painted the lavender color of the sky behind the sun over most of the canvas. He wrapped the top and left side of this painting in a canopy of warm orange, yellow, and rust-colored tones. The high point of view, the cool dark blue skiff, and the sun's hot orange reflection lead our eyes into Monet's vision of an open harbor.

Using jagged brush strokes and streaks of paint, Monet quickly captured the changing color of the light as the sun fell in the evening sky. Many art critics who saw this painting for the first time were outraged by its sketchy, unfinished quality. They could not see that Monet had unlocked the secret of a blazing sunset.

In this painting of Etretat, Monet captured the fury of a sea so dangerous-looking that it prevents the fishermen from setting out to work.

THE SHORE OF THE TURQUOISE SEA, 1878
Albert Bierstadt, American (1830–1902), Oil on canvas, 42½" x 64½"

*A*lbert Bierstadt had the good fortune of beginning his career just when the U.S. government sent a mapping expedition to the Rocky Mountains. He joined the team, and gained access to the subject he would paint for the rest of his life—the grandeur of natural formations. Bierstadt treated art as a business and created paintings that were collected by wealthy industrialists who viewed them as symbols of power.

In this painting, Bierstadt depicted the overwhelming, destructive power of a tropical hurricane. The immense mast of a wrecked ship is carried like a feather by a huge wave. The shallow foreground seems to crowd us against the jagged rocks, creating a sense that the great wave is about to engulf us. There is no human figure to compare to the size of the wave, but we sense it. The water has surged so high that it becomes translucent. Turquoise reflections illuminate the blue-black sea and the slippery rocks along the beach. The color seems even more brilliant in contrast to the inky black clouds. Bierstadt painted every detail, from the ropes on the broken mast to the delicate tracery on seashells. This painting seems more real than reality, and every inch displays the painter's technical gifts.

A detail shows that the colors Bierstadt painted to form the towering curve of the translucent wave are actually strands of seaweed.

During his lifetime, Bierstadt was often criticized because he exaggerated nature's glories to appeal to his patrons. But his talent for visualizing a disappearing world has found a new audience among historians and environmentalists in the twentieth century.

WOMEN BATHING, 1885
Paul Gauguin, French (1848–1903), Oil on canvas, 15" x 18¼"

In 1883, Paul Gauguin left his job as a successful insurance broker to become an artist, and began a life of poverty. By 1885, his wife, Mette, had been forced to return to her family in Copenhagen with their five children, while Gauguin struggled to survive in Paris. The only job he could find—gluing posters onto walls and fences—paid five francs a day. Fortunately, a friend invited him to Dieppe, on the English Channel, where he spent the summer painting.

Six years as a sailor had provided Gauguin with an education in the ocean's changing forms and colors. In *Women Bathing*, he captured the action of a wave breaking on the beach. Gauguin painted a broad area of clear green color for the sea beyond the breakers. Closer to land, the shallow water becomes yellow shot with blue, reflecting the sand below and the sky above. The curve of the breaking wave is formed with lavender, pink, and green shadows. Three bathers stand in the shallows, holding hands in anticipation of the cold water about to hit their sun-warmed bodies. The fourth woman stands back, keeping a watchful eye on the wave.

Gauguin composed this painting in three distinct bands of color punctuated by the triangular arrangement of figures in the foreground and sailboats on the horizon. The angled arms of the women are echoed by the shapes of the sails—and the still figures stand in contrast to the turbulent water at their feet. During this difficult period in his life, Gauguin found enjoyment in the seaside climate and he expressed his pleasure through the use of sparkling colors.

Using a pen made from a reed, the great artist Vincent van Gogh shaped rhythmical patterns for the water and waves in this ink drawing.

THE ENGLISH CHANNEL AT GRANDCAMP, 1885

Georges Seurat, French (1859–1891), Oil on canvas, 26" x 32½"

Standing guard at an army fort overlooking the English Channel, Georges Seurat observed the changing light, color, and seaside weather. In the moist ocean climate, Seurat noticed, the hazy white light softened colors and shapes. He stored these scenes in his memory and recalled the images to reinvent the effects of outdoor light with paint.

Seurat had studied scientific theories about the physical properties of light, and found that if he placed two colors next to each other, he could create the effect of a third color—and sometimes a fourth. Instead of mixing paint colors on his palette, Seurat painted tiny colored dots on the canvas. To the viewer, the dots seem to blend together. He created shimmering paintings that appeared to be the source—not merely pictures—of light. Seurat's technique for applying color has become known as *pointillism*, a word that means painting with dots.

In this picture, Seurat built the forms of the building, a fence, and bushes in the foreground by painting shadowy tones first. Then he added touches of soft yellow and orange; next, chalky-looking blue and green. Seurat created a luminous cloud of warm, hazy color around the buildings and jetty in the background. Over this, he painted little dabs of lavender, yellow, orange, and blue to create the effect of flickering sunlight. He unified the picture by using the same tones throughout, adding more and more white to the colors as they reach the horizon.

Seurat was driven by his intellect and a desire to merge art and science. He controlled every inch of his canvases, and was opposed to "artistic accidents." Seurat even painted his picture frames with the same colors as those in the paintings.

Seurat used vertical forms—the lighthouse, flagpole, smokestacks, and the stanchion in the foreground—in contrast to the horizontal bands that form the sky, water, and land.

28

EIGHT BELLS, 1886
Winslow Homer, American (1836–1910), Oil on canvas, 25" x 30"

In 1849, Winslow Homer's father lost the family's money in the California gold rush. Winslow went to work as a commercial artist at the age of nineteen and became a successful illustrator and Civil War correspondent. By the time the war was over, he had earned enough money to paint full-time.

In Paris, Homer studied art at the same time Courbet and Monet were creating new ways to express the beauty of natural light. He returned from France, built a studio on the coast of Maine, and began painting his own American view of life.

The pounding fury of storms at sea and the mariners who worked among these powerful forces intrigued Homer. In *Eight Bells,* he portrays two men who have emerged from below deck after a fierce storm. The sun breaks through steep cumulus clouds; the wind whips the sea into foaming swells. Against this background of nature's fury, Homer depicts the sailors calmly taking navigational readings with instruments known as octants.

Homer saw the sky, water, and light as masses of color. He translated the mingling of atmospheric moisture with windswept seawater into one system of cold gray-green color and white light. With bold patches of paint, he created the effect of the churning water and rapidly moving clouds. In contrast, he clearly defined the figures with lines, highlights, and shadows to shape their soaking-wet slickers.

Homer "framed" the mariners with the ship's hull and rigging. He separated the men and their ship from sky and water to suggest that man can endure— but not control—nature's power.

The gray paper that Homer used for this charcoal-and-chalk drawing conveys the tone of both the sky and the water.

30

SEINE BARGES, 1906
André Derain, French (1880–1954), Oil on canvas, 31⅜" x 38½"

The Seine river snakes through France for five hundred miles and makes three loops as it winds through Paris. André Derain had a studio on an island in the third loop, where he often painted the working life on the great river.

Derain challenges us to look at an everyday subject and discover the extraordinary. His viewpoint—looking down from a bridge high above the water—hurls us into this urban riverscape. We can almost hear the groaning oars as two barges slip under a bridge. Brilliant winter sun casts an icy blue shadow on the water. A billowing puff of steam from the engine hangs frozen above the river.

Derain had observed that in glaring sunlight, shadows are not black or gray—they can be many different colors, depending on the nearby reflections. He painted a pale blue shadow of the barges to intensify the reflection of light on water and made the darkest shadows a bright blue. Using large brushes and only four colors—yellow, blue, red, and green—Derain applied slabs of paint to suggest the cargo and the toiling oarsmen.

Bold outlines emphasize the geometrical blocks of color and draw our attention to the way Derain designed this painting. He placed the two barges at a steep angle with one cut off at the edge to create a sense of movement. More sharp angles in the oars and the triangular sail add to the effect. Derain painted the sun's reflections on the churning water into more than half of the canvas to complete this picture of a brilliant but freezing light on a winter day.

In this close-up, we see that Derain painted blocks of color rather than lines or shading to suggest, rather than describe, the forms of the mariners and their cargo.

SUMMER AFTERNOON, 1906–8

Frank W. Benson, American (1862–1951), Oil on canvas, 30½" x 39½"

Frank Benson studied painting for two years in Paris. He admired the way Monet and Renoir interpreted the play of light on water in their seascape paintings. In 1885, he returned to New England and began to use the same brilliant colors in his own work.

Benson also taught at the School of the Museum of Fine Arts in Boston. In summer, he and his family moved to an island farmhouse in Maine, where they enjoyed the beauty of the clear sunlight and the freedom of outdoor life at the ocean. Benson created many paintings of his children against the pristine waters of the North Atlantic.

This painting is like a moment suspended in time. Pink reflections on the clouds and sails tell us that evening is approaching. Benson painted contrasting tones of purple, yellow, and pink against turquoise blue to create sparkling reflections on the water. He applied the paint in thick layers; while it was wet, he pulled up the texture of waves using stiff bristle brushes.

Benson formed a striking composition through the placement of the figures and boats. His daughters Elisabeth and Eleanor look up from their conversation, while Sylvia tugs at her braids. The dog sights something beyond the edge of the canvas. His placement and alert gaze connect the figures in a circular arrangement. Yellow reflections and pale blue shadows on the girls' dresses relate the figures to the colors of the sea and sky.

In *Summer Afternoon*, Benson expressed his personal vision of the ocean's beauty — and his great happiness in his beloved children and his island home.

William Zorach left large areas of white paper unpainted to form the carrousel horses, the deck, and the clouds in this watercolor.

34

SAILING, 1911
Edward Hopper, American (1882–1967), Oil on canvas, 24" x 29"

In 1913, Edward Hopper sold this painting at an exhibition in New York City that was attended by four hundred thousand people. It was his only sale for more than ten years. During this period, he supported himself as an illustrator and painted during summer vacations in Maine. Hopper's first one-man exhibit in 1924 was a success, and afterward, he began creating stark paintings that often make us think we are seeing an ordinary place or event for the last time.

In *Sailing*, Hopper expressed a feeling of loneliness through his use of design and color. The boat seems very small compared to the size of the two figures and the large wave. We can tell from the foaming wake that the wind is

Hopper was a gifted printmaker as well as a painter. In this etching, the velvety black background forms a sharp contrast to the white sail and the water.

strong and the boat is moving rapidly. Hopper cropped off the top of the sail to emphasize the vastness of sky and water compared to the little sailboat.

Using a small range of toned-down colors, Hopper built on the story he began with the composition. He painted a reddish color on the boom to define the sail's steep angle under the power of the wind. He unified the boat and its sails with the same pale yellow to emphasize the sense of speed. The cold gray-green color of the sea and the flat, metallic-looking sky suggest that the weather is about to change for the worse. The figures are indicated with blocks of neutral colors punctuated by a bright patch of red paint. Hopper painted large, unbroken areas of color with only a few shadows to focus our attention on the two sailors at sea, far away from land.

THE COVE, 1936

Lucien Lévy-Dhurmer, French, born in Algeria (1865–1953), Pastel on paper, 30" x 24³/₄"

The deep water of the ocean is secret and mysterious, like the mind. When it is impossible to imagine what someone we love is thinking, we try to guess, and sometimes enter a dreamlike state. In *The Cove*, Lucien Lévy-Dhurmer explored his dreams and created a powerful image of two opposites: the height of the cliffs and the depth of the sea.

Craggy cliffs rise steeply from the tranquil sea, shutting out the rest of the world. The viewer seems to perch on the edge, with no access to the water far below. Lévy-Dhurmer created an air of mystery by frosting the icy-looking rocks with pink highlights, and with shadows of turquoise and lavender. A glimmer of light on the water comes from an invisible source. It appears that time has stopped somewhere between night and daybreak.

Lévy-Dhurmer painted *The Cove* in pastel—a material he used to its greatest advantage. Pastel is made of pigment ground into a fine powder, and formed into a stick with a small amount of gum arabic. The colors are pure, and range from delicate tints to the most brilliant shades. Unlike wet paint colors, which can be mixed before they are applied, pastel tones are built up in layers directly on the paper. The artist must handle his painting carefully because the color is like powder. Until it is protected with a coat of fixative, the color can blow away with the wind. In this ghostly scene, Lévy-Dhurmer seems to be searching through his dreams and memories to re-create the feeling of a haunting moment that was important to him.

THE CASINO AT NICE, NIGHT, 1935–36
Raoul Dufy, French (1877–1953), Watercolor on paper, 19³/₄" x 25⁵/₈"

Le Havre, where Raoul Dufy grew up and began painting, is a coastal city in the north of France. Boats in the harbor were his first subject, and watercolor the first paint he used. The interplay of color and reflected light at the water's edge formed his earliest impressions and occupied him as an artist all of his life.

Dufy had a passion for beauty and for joyous times. With a sure hand and observant eyes, he made this sparkling painting of the Bay of Angels in his adopted city of Nice, in the south of France. He spent many happy winters here and preferred the clear, almost metallic quality of the southern light to the foggy gray skies of the north.

Boldly, spontaneously, he covered most of the roughly textured white paper with translucent ultramarine blue paint, leaving the shape of the domed casino and the lights uncovered. The thin wash of blue allowed the texture of the white paper to create a shimmering effect. While paint and paper were still wet, he brushed on the yellow reflections of city lights on the sky; the viridian green lawn, which becomes a mist of color where it meets the sea; and the rose-colored beach that merges with the still water. Dufy waited until the paper was bone dry before painting in the luminous yellow lights and the palm trees.

Over this freely painted image, Dufy used dark blue paint and a dry brush to quickly draw dozens of little chairs and an ornamental railing — and created a touch of realism to define the water's edge.

41

THE PIGEONS, 1957
Pablo Picasso, Spanish (1881–1973), Oil on canvas, 39³/₈" x 31⁷/₈"

Picasso said, "Every child is an artist. The problem is how to remain an artist when we grow up. When I was their age, I could draw like Raphael, but it took me a lifetime to draw like a child." Picasso achieved his ambition in the last two decades of his long career as an artist.

In 1957, Picasso was seventy-six years old. He lived in a sprawling mansion overlooking the Mediterranean Sea, where he painted subjects important to his personal happiness: his wife, his children, his home, and his pets. The great artist Henri Matisse had given Picasso a pair of Milanese pigeons, which quickly raised their own family.

In this picture, which he called an "interior landscape," Picasso expressed his great happiness through his use of bright colors and freely painted forms. He painted an open window looking onto the sparkling azure sea as a tribute to his friend, Matisse, who had used this motif many times in his own paintings. Picasso framed the ocean with a sun-drenched wall the color of homemade butter. He applied bold strokes of orange and white almost like finger paints. With large brushes and thick paint, Picasso drew tropical plants, sunflowers, and a decorative window grating. He painted two of the birds strutting and preening, keenly observed by their nestmates.

Picasso is regarded as the most innovative painter of the twentieth century because he never stopped finding new ways to express his vision as an artist. He said that to search was nothing—it is what you *discover* that makes the difference.

*Picasso captured the pigeons'
ruffled feathers by using a few rapid
strokes of his big brushes.*

42

TO THE ISLAND, 1982
Jennifer Bartlett, American (born 1941), Oil on canvas, 84" x 120"

As a young painter, Jennifer Bartlett was so interested in the work of other artists that she sometimes could not decide what to paint. She often solved this problem by painting the same subject in many ways, using different materials and techniques. Through the physical labor of painting, her best ideas emerged.

Bartlett was inspired by *Thirty-six Views of Mount Fuji,* a series of wood-block prints created by the great Japanese artist Hokusai one hundred fifty years earlier. She visited Japan to see this famous region, which has attracted artists for centuries.

Bartlett takes a point of view that puts the observer in a tiny boat, and creates an awareness of movement and the passage of time. We are so close to the water that it seems that the little boat is traveling dangerously fast to reach the island before a hurricane begins. Brilliant reflections next to the island and the stark white of the sky above suggest the limitless sea beyond the horizon. Bartlett worked from photographs to paint the waves, clouds, and shadows in ragged, almost abstract patches of cold color—white, gray, blue-gray, blue, and blue-black. At first it seems like a paint-by-numbers kit until we realize that she has adapted the bold, flat colors of small Japanese prints to a ten-foot-wide oil painting and transformed the legendary shape of Mount Fuji into an imaginary island.

The picture on the right is one of ten different paintings of the island theme by Bartlett. She began with an idea from another time and a different culture to create her personal vision of a mythical mountain rising from the sea.

A Japanese artist named Hokusai created a fierce ocean storm with a towering wave that dwarfs Mount Fuji in the background. In the 1830s, he created a series of thirty-six wood-block prints of the famous mountain.

Glossary and Index

PAINT: Artists have used different kinds of paint, depending on the materials that were available to them and the effects they wished to produce in their work.

Different kinds of paint are similar in the way they are made.

1. Paint is made by combining finely powdered pigment with a vehicle. A vehicle is a substance that evenly disperses the color and produces a consistency that can be like mayonnaise and sometimes as thick as peanut butter. The kind of vehicle used sometimes gives the paint its name. Pigment is the raw material that gives paint its color. Pigments are made from natural minerals and from man-made chemical compounds.

2. Paint is made thinner or thicker with a substance called a medium. Different paints require the use of mediums appropriate to their composition.

3. A solvent must be used by the painter to clean the paint from brushes, tools, and the hands. The solvent must be appropriate for the composition of the paint.

OIL PAINT, 14, 16, 20, 22, 24, 26, 28, 30, 32, 34, 36, 42, 44: Pigment is combined with an oil vehicle (usually linseed or poppy oil). The medium chosen by most artists is linseed oil. The solvent is turpentine. Oil paint dries slowly, which enables the artist to work on a painting for a long time. Some painters mix other materials, such as pumice or marble dust, into oil paint to produce thick layers of color. Oil paint is never mixed with water. Oil paint has been used since the fifteenth century. Until the early nineteenth century, artists or their assistants ground the pigment and combined the ingredients of paint in their studios. In 1840, paint became available in flexible tin tubes (like toothpaste tubes).

WATERCOLOR, 10, 18, 34, 40: Pigment is combined with gum arabic, a water-based vehicle. Water is both the medium and the solvent. Watercolor paint now comes ready to use in tubes (moist) or in cakes (dry). With transparent watercolor, unlike other painting techniques, white paint is not used to lighten the colors. Watercolor paint is thinned with water, and areas of paper are often left uncovered to produce highlights. Watercolor paint was first used 37,000 years ago by cave dwellers who created the first wall paintings.

PASTEL, 38: (1) A soft crayon made of powdered pigment, chalk, water, and mixed with a small amount of gum. (2) A painting or sketch made with this type of crayon.

PATRON, 24: One who supports the arts or an individual artist.

PERSPECTIVE, 10, 14, 22: A method of representing people, places, and things in a painting or drawing to make them appear solid or three-dimensional, rather than flat. Six basic rules of perspective are used in Western art.

1. People in a painting appear larger when near and gradually become smaller as they get farther away.

2. People in the foreground overlap the activity behind them.

3. People become closer together as they get farther away.

4. People in the distance appear higher up in the picture than those in the foreground.

5. Colors are brighter and shadows are stronger in the foreground. Colors and shadows are paler and softer in the background. This effect is also called *aerial perspective*.

6. Lines that in real life are parallel (such as the line of a ceiling and the line of a floor) are drawn at an angle, and the lines meet at the "horizon line," which represents the eye level of the viewer.

Painters have used these methods to depict objects in space since the fifteenth century. But many twentieth-century artists do not use perspective. An artist might emphasize color, line, or shape to express an idea, instead of depicting a realistic space.

Picasso, Pablo, 42

Pigeons, The, 42

PLASTER, 8: A chalky white powder that is mixed with water to form a thick paste that dries to a hard finish. Plaster used as a surface for wall painting is often a mixture of lime and gypsum.

POINTILLISM, 28: A word that means to paint with individual dots of color rather than brush strokes.

PRINT, 36, 44: One of many images created by mechanical means from the same original. Prints can be made from a metal plate (etching, aquatint, engraving), from a wood block (wood-block print), from a silk gauze (silk screen print), or from a stone (lithograph).

Sailing, 36

Sanctuary by the Sea, A, 8

Seaport with Ulysses Returning Chryseius to Her Father, 14

SEASCAPE, 8, 16, 34: A painting, drawing, print, or photograph in which the sea is the most important subject.

Seine Barges, 32

Seurat, Georges, 28 (Pronounced Zhorzheh Suhr-rah)

SHADOW, 14, 26, 28, 30, 32, 34, 36, 38, 44: An area made darker than its surroundings because direct light does not reach it.

Shore of the Turquoise Sea, The, 24

SILHOUETTE, 22: An image of a person or an object that consists of the outline of its shape in a solid color.

SKETCH, 10, 18, 22: A quickly made drawing.

Summer Afternoon, 34

TEXTURE, 16, 20, 34, 40: The surface quality of a painting. For example, an oil painting could have a thin, smooth surface texture or a thick, rough surface texture.

To the Island, 44

TONE, 20, 22, 28, 34, 38: The sensation of an overall coloration in a painting. For example, an artist might begin by painting the entire picture in shades of greenish gray. After more colors are applied using transparent glazes, shadows, and highlights, the mass of greenish gray color underneath will show through and create an even tone, or "tonal harmony."

One of the ways that painters working with opaque colors can achieve the same effect is by adding one color, such as green, to every other color on their palette. This makes all of the colors seem more alike, or "harmonious." The effect of tonal harmony is part of the artist's vision and begins with the first brush strokes.

Tours Sunset, 18

TRANSPARENT, 18: Allowing light to pass through so colors underneath can be seen. (The opposite of OPAQUE.)

Turner, Joseph Mallord William, 16, 18

TURPENTINE: A strong-smelling solvent made from pine sap; used in oil painting. (See PAINT: OIL PAINT.)

UNDERPAINTING, 20: The initial stages of a painting. Artists often first paint the entire picture in neutral colors, such as brown, gray, blue, or green. Over the underpainting, they build up the colors, shadows, and textures, letting areas of the underpainting show through to create a consistent tone throughout. See TONE.

VELLUM, 10: Fine calfskin or goatskin formerly used in illuminated manuscripts. Heavy-weight paper, also called vellum, is now used for books created by artists. Vellum is also called parchment.

Whale Ship, The, 16

Women Bathing, 26

Credits